Laura Elizabeth Howe Richards

Narcissa

The Road to Rome

Laura Elizabeth Howe Richards

Narcissa
The Road to Rome

ISBN/EAN: 9783744677790

Printed in Europe, USA, Canada, Australia, Japan

Cover: Foto ©Thomas Meinert / pixelio.de

More available books at **www.hansebooks.com**

NARCISSA

IN VERONA

NARCISSA

OR

THE ROAD TO ROME

IN VERONA

BY

LAURA E. RICHARDS

AUTHOR OF "CAPTAIN JANUARY," "MELODY,"
"QUEEN HILDEGARDE," ETC.

ELEVENTH THOUSAND

BOSTON
ESTES & LAURIAT
1894

𝔘𝔫𝔦𝔳𝔢𝔯𝔰𝔦𝔱𝔶 𝔓𝔯𝔢𝔰𝔰:
John Wilson and Son, Cambridge, U.S.A.

CONTENTS.

694956

NARCISSA.

NARCISSA.

THE ROAD TO ROME.

Part I.

DREAMING.

NARCISSA was sitting in the doorway, feeding the young turkeys. It was the back door of the old gray house, — no one would have thought of sitting in the front doorway, — and there were crooked flag-stones leading up to it, cracked and seamed, with grass growing in the cracks. Close by the door-post, against which the girl was leaning, stood a great bush of tansy, with waving feathery leaves and yellow blossoms, like small gold buttons. Narcissa was very fond of this tansy-bush, and liked to pluck a leaf and crush it in her hands, to bring out the keen, wholesome smell. She had one in her hand now, and was wondering if ever any one had a dress of green velvet, tansy-color, with gold buttons. The minister's wife once had a bow of green velvet on her black straw bonnet, and Narcissa had loved to look at it, and to wish it were somewhere else, with things that belonged to it. She often thought of splendid clothes, though she had never seen anything finer than the black silk of the minister's wife, and that always made her think of a newly-blacked stove. When she was younger, she had made a romance about every scrap of silk or satin in the crazy-quilt that Aunt Pinker's daughter, the milliner, had sent her one Christmas. The gown she had had out of that yellow satin — it did her good to think about it even now! — and there was a scrap of pale pink silk which came — was it really nothing but fancy? — from a long, trailing robe, trimmed with filmy lace (the lace in the story-papers was always filmy), in which she had passed many happy, dreamy hours.

It never occurred to Narcissa that she needed no fine clothes to set off her beauty; in truth, she never dreamed that she had any beauty. Color meant so much to her, that she had always accepted the general verdict that she was " pindlin'-lookin'," and joined sincerely in the chorus of praise which always greeted the rosy cheeks and solid-looking yellow hair of Delilah Parshley, who lived at the next house below the old gray one.

Yet it was true that Narcissa had no need of finery ; and it was a pretty picture she made, sitting in the doorway, leaning against the door-post. Her hair was nearly black, with no gloss or sparkle, only a soft, dusky cloudiness. It curled in little rings about her broad, low forehead, and round her soft, pale cheeks. Her eyes were dusky, too, but more gray than brown, and the only vivid color was in the scarlet line of her lips. There was nothing unhealthy in her clear pallor, no hint of sallowness, but a soft, white glow. The nostrils of her little straight nose were cut high, which gave them a look of being always slightly dilated; this caused the neighbors to say that Narcissa White was proud, though dear knew what she had to be proud of. As for her dress, it was of blue jean, a good deal faded, but all the better for that; and her white apron, though coarse, was spotless and carefully starched.

The turkeys seemed to approve of her appearance, for they gathered eagerly round her, trying to get their beaks into the dish she held, gobbling and fluttering, and making a great commotion. Narcissa was fond of the turkeys, and had names for all her favorites. The finest young gobbler was called Black Diamond, and he was apt to take unfair advantage of his mistress's partiality, and to get more than his share. So noisy they all were, that Narcissa did not hear the sound of approaching footsteps, nor know that some one had spoken to her twice in vain, and was now standing in silent amusement, watching the struggle for food.

It was a young man who had come so lightly up the steps of the old house that no sound had been heard. He had gone first to the front door, but his knock had brought no answer, and catching the flutter of Narcissa's apron he had come round to the back porch and was standing within three feet of the girl and her clamorous brood.

A very young man, hardly more than a boy, yet with a steady, manly look in his blue eyes, which contradicted the boyish curves of cheek and chin. He was plainly but neatly dressed, and he carried in one hand a small satchel, such as travelling agents affect. His eyes were bright and quick, and glanced about with keen interest, taking in every outline of the house, but coming always back to the girl who sat in the doorway, and who was unlike any girl he had seen before. The house was dim and gaunt, with a look of great age. One did not often, in this part of the country, see such tall doors, such quaint chimneys, such irregular outlines of roof and gable. The green-painted front door, with its brass knocker, and its huge, old-world hinges, seemed to him a great curiosity; so did the high stone steps, whose forlorn dignity suffered perpetual insult from the malapert weeds and grasses that laughed and nodded through the cracks and seams.

And in the dim, sunken doorway sat this girl, herself all soft and shadowy, with a twilight look in her eyes and in her dusky hair. The turkeys were the only part of it all that seemed to belong to the sort of life about here, the hard, bustling life of New England farm-people, such as he had seen at the other houses along the way. If it were not for the turkeys, he felt that he should hardly find courage to speak, for fear it might all melt away into the gathering twilight, — house, maiden, and all, — and leave nothing but the tall elms that waved their spectral arms over the sunken roofs.

As it was, however, — as the turkeys were making such a racket that the girl would never become aware of his presence unless he asserted himself in some way, — he stepped boldly forward and lifted his hat, for he had been taught good manners, if he was a tree-agent.

"Excuse me, lady," he said. "Is this the road to Rome?"

Narcissa started violently, and came out of her dream. She had actually been dressed in the green velvet, and was fastening the last gold button, ready to step into the chariot that was waiting for her, — she loved the word chariot, though the pictures in the Bible made her feel uncertain about the manner of riding in one, — and to drive along the road, the road to Rome. How strange that at this very moment some one should ask about the road!

She raised her eyes, still shining with the dream-light, and looked attentively at the stranger.

"Yes, sir," she answered. "This is the road, — the road to Rome. But it's a long way from here," she added, rousing herself, and rising from her seat. "Shoo!

go away, now;" and she waved a signal of dismissal
with her apron which the turkeys understood, and at
sight of which they withdrew, not without angry
cluckings and gobblings directed at the disturber of
their evening meal.

"Won't you set down and rest a spell? It's ben
real hot to-day, though it's some cooler now."

"It has so!" assented the young man, taking off his
hat again to wipe his brow, and dropping his satchel
on the doorstep.

"I should be pleased to set a few minutes, if I'm
not intruding. And do you suppose I could have a
drink of water, if it would n't be too much trouble?"

Narcissa went away without a word, and brought
back the water, ice-cold and clear as crystal, in a queer
brown mug with a twisted handle, and an inscription
in white letters.

"I'm sorry I have n't got a glass," she said. "But
the water is good."

The young man drank deeply, and then looked curi-
ously at the mug. "I'd rather have this than a glass,"
he said. "It's quite a curiosity, ain't it? 'Be Merry!'
Well, that's a good sentiment, I'm sure. Thank you,
lady. I'm ever so much obliged."

"You no need to," responded Narcissa, civilly.

"I — I don't suppose you want any trees or plants
to set out, do you?" said the stranger. "I am travelling for a house near Portland, and I've got some first-
rate things, — real chances, I call 'em."

"I — guess not," said Narcissà, with an apprehensive glance over her shoulder. "I only keep house for the man here, — he 's my father's uncle, — and he don't buy such things. I wish " — she sighed, and looked longingly at the black satchel. "I suppose you 've got roses, have you, and all kinds of flowers ? "

"I should think so!" replied the youth, proudly. "Our house is the greatest one in the State for roses. Let me show you some pictures." He opened the satchel and took out a black order-book filled with brilliant pictures.

"Oh!" cried Narcissa, "I — I guess I 'd better not look at 'em. I don't believe he 'd like it. Not but what I 'm just as much obliged to you," she added, hastily.

But the stranger had already opened the book.

"Just look here, lady," he said. "Why, it can't do no manner of hurt for you to look at them. Just see here! Here 's the Jacqueminot rose, the finest in the world, some folks think. Why, we 've got beds and beds of it. Splendid grower, and sweet — well there! I can't give you any idea of it. Cornelia Cook! that 's a great rose nowadays. And here 's a white blush, that looks for all the world like — "

Here he stopped suddenly; for it was Narcissa's cheek that the rose was like, he thought, and it came to him suddenly that he did not want to say such things to this girl.

The girl at the house below, when he had paid her

compliments, had laughed in his face, well pleased, and seemed to ask for more; but she was an ordinary girl, like other folks. This soft, shadowy maiden might shrink away, and vanish in the dusky porch, if he should touch her rudely.

He need have had no fear, for Narcissa would hardly have heard or understood his compliment. She was gazing with hungry eyes at the bright pictures, drinking in every shade of crimson and scarlet and gold.

"Oh, stop!" she cried eagerly. "Oh, may I read about that one? Ain't it beautiful! May I?"

"Well, I should think you might!" replied the gallant agent, holding the book toward her. "Here, lean right over me; I'd like to read it too."

"'This grand rose,'" Narcissa read aloud, "'has created an epoch in rose-growing. Of free habit and luxurious growth, the plants form the most splendid ornament of garden or hot-house. The beautiful, perfectly-shaped flowers show a marvellous blending of colors, in which a rich apricot predominates, shading into light pink, bright canary, and pale yellow. The outer petals are grandly recurved, forming a fine contrast to the Camellia-like inner petals. With its rare and exquisite fragrance, its bold and beautiful foliage, and the unparalleled profusion with which its splendid blossoms are borne, we claim that this rose is absolutely *without a rival.*'"

Narcissa drew a long breath and looked up, her

eyes full of awe and admiration. "Ain't that elegant?" she said simply. "They have great writers there, don't they?"

The youth smiled, as he thought of little Mr. Bimsey, who "got up" the catalogues and kept the accounts; then, reminded by this and by the fading light that he had still a good way to go before nightfall, he added, rising reluctantly from his seat, —

"I must be going, I guess. You haven't any notion how far it might be to Rome, have you, lady?"

Narcissa shook her head.

"It's a long way," she said. "When Uncle Pinker goes there with the turkeys in the fall, it takes him the whole day to go and come."

"You haven't got a map of the county?" persisted the youth. "I'd ought to have one myself, and I guess I shall have to get me one. I'm a stranger in these parts."

Narcissa shook her head again. "We haven't got any kind of a map, as I know of," she said; but next moment her face brightened. "We've got a picture of Rome," she said, — "a real handsome picture. Would you like to see it?"

"Well, if it ain't too much trouble."

Narcissa led the way into the house, cautioning the stranger to tread softly. "Uncle Pinker is asleep," she said. "He's real old, and he sleeps in the afternoon, most times. He's so deaf, he wouldn't hear you

most likely, but you never can count on deef folks.
Not but what he'd be pleased to see you," she
added, with a doubtful look at a closed door as she
passed it.

"I'd ought to make you acquainted with my name,
seem's though," said the agent, following her into a
dim, dreary room. "My name's Patten, — Romulus
Patten." He paused, and then went on: "Folks
always ask how I got my name, so I get into the way
of firing right ahead before they ask. My mother got
it out of the history book. She was a great hand
for history, my mother was. It seems queer, my
going to Rome, don't it? They made consid'able fun
about it, down to our place, but I'm used to that,
and don't mind it."

There was no answering gleam in Narcissa's lovely
eyes. "Romulus? was he in the Revolution?" she asked.
"I had to leave school before we got through history.
I'd only got as far as the Battle of Lexington, when
Aunt Pinker died, and I had to come and keep house
for Uncle Pinker. It was real interestin'," she added,
with a little sigh of regret, " I wish 't I could have
finished history."

Romulus Patten flushed with shame and anger, — not
at the girl, but at the sordid people who had kept her
in ignorance. He had gone through General History
himself, and having a good memory, considered himself very well up in such matters. When he came back,

he thought, perhaps he might manage to stop a spell, and tell her a little about things. Romulus in the Revolution! it was a scandalous shame, and she so sweet and pretty!

But here was the picture of Rome, and Narcissa turning with gentle pride to introduce him to it.

"Ain't it handsome?" she cried with enthusiasm. "I do like to look at it the most of anything, seem's though. I think you're real fortunate to be going there, Mr. — Mr. Patten."

She was silent, gazing with delight that was fresh every time her eyes rested on the beloved picture; and Romulus Patten was silent too.

What was it he saw?

A steel engraving, dim and gray, like the house, like the walls on which it hung; framed in dingy gold, spotted and streaked. Within, as in a dull mirror, appeared towers and temples, columned porticos and triumphal arches: the whole seemed to be steeped in pale sunshine; in the background rose a monstrous shape which Romulus' practised eye, familiar with the illustrations in the General History, recognized as the Coliseum. "That's Rome!" said Narcissa, softly. "Ain't it elegant?"

The young man glanced at her, with a light of sympathetic amusement in his eyes. This was her little joke; he had hardly thought she would make jokes, she was so quiet. But the smile faded into a look of bewilderment, which quickly strove to efface itself; for Narcissa was not in jest. She was gazing at the picture with a rapt look, with almost passionate enjoyment. She had forgotten him for the moment, and had entered the city of her dreams as she so often entered it, robed in velvet and satin (it was the tansy-colored velvet this time, and the buttons were very splendid indeed, and she had a bunch of roses in her hand), riding in a chariot. She was passing under those wonderful arches; that soft, mysterious sun-shine wrapped her in a cloud of glory. Presently she would meet other beings, splendidly dressed like herself, who would greet her with smiles, and tell her of other strange and beautiful things that she was going to see. Ah, to be in Rome! to be really going there!

"Ain't it handsome?" she repeated, turning her soft eyes on her companion. "You're real fortunate to be going there."

Romulus Patten stammered. "You — you're sure that is Rome?" he said. "This same Rome, down east here? It don't hardly seem just like a down-east place, does it?"

The soft eyes grew wide, and the lips smiled a little. "Why, it says so!" said Narcissa. "See here, right under the picture, 'Rome.' So it couldn't be any place else, could it?"

"I — I suppose not," murmured Romulus, hang-

ing his head, like one found in an unpardonable
ignoiance.

"I hope to go there some day," the girl went on.
"It's never been so I could, yet; and folks don't go
much from about here. Ain't it queer? They'll go the
other way, to Tupham, and Cyrus, and other places
that's just like — like to home here, — " and she gave
a little disparaging glance along the bleak road, with
its straggling willows and birches, — "and there's
scarcely anybody goes to Rome. And it like that!"
she added, with another look of loving reverence at
the old picture.

"You said something about your uncle going," sug-
gested Romulus. "Has n't he ever told you about the
place, — whether it's like the picture?"

Narcissa shook he head. "I asked him last time
he come back," she said. "I've asked him two or
three times; but all he does is nod his head and laugh,
the way he has. He ain't one to talk, Uncle Pinker
ain't. He goes to Rome once every fall, when he kills
the turkeys. The biggest part of 'em goes the other
way, to Tupham and on beyond, but he allers takes
some portion to Rome. He says they're great on
turkeys there. I should think they would be,
should n't you?"

This was a long speech for Narcissa, and she re-
lapsed into silence and the picture.

"And you live all alone here with a deef old man

who don't talk?" said Romulus Patten. "Excuse me, Miss — well, you have n't told me your name, have you?" and he laughed a little.

"Narcissa," was the reply. "Narcissa White."

"Thank you!" said the well-mannered Romulus. "You live all alone with him, and don't see no company? It's lonesome for you, ain't it?"

"I — don't — know," Narcissa answered thoughtfully. "I never thought much about it's bein' lonesome. I have the turkeys, and they're a good deal of company: and I — I think about things." A faint color stole into her clear white cheek, as she remembered the velvet gown. She supposed a man would consider such thoughts "triflin'."

"Don't you see anything of the neighbors?" the young man persisted. "There's a young lady down at the next house, half a mile below here, — wide-awake looking girl, with yeller hair and red cheeks, looks some like a geranium; don't you know her?"

"That's Delilah Parshley!" said Narcissa. "She's real handsome, don't you think so? No, I don't see her, only to meetin' sometimes. I guess she don't care to go much with folks up this way. Her friends is mostly the other way, on the Tupham road. Their house sets on the corner, you know."

Narcissa did not know — how should she? — that Delilah Parshley and the other girls of her sort considered her "a little wanting," because she was silent, and never seemed interested in the doings of the neighbors, or of such stray travellers as came along the road to Rome. She felt kindly toward the Parshleys, as toward all the "meetin' folks;" but she rarely held speech with them, and was "gettin' as dumb as the old man was deef," the neighbors were beginning to say.

"But have n't you got any folks of your own?" this persistent young man went on. "I — I hope I 'm not too forth-puttin', Miss White, but I 'd like to know."

"I 'm sure you 're real kind to ask!" replied Narcissa, who was not used to having any one care to ask her questions.

"Yes, I 've got *some* folks. Father 's livin', but he 's married again, and there 's more children, and he was glad to have me find a chance; and it was so that I was glad, too," she added, with no resentment in her tone, but a touch of sadness, which made the ready color come into those tell-tale cheeks of Romulus Patten.

"It ain't right," he said hotly. "I 'll be switched if it 's right. Ain't there a better chance you could get, somewheres round here, if you don't feel to go fur away? If you did feel to make a change, there 's lots of chances down our way. I 'd be real pleased to be of assistance, if there was any ways I could; I would, now, Miss White."

Narcissa looked a little alarmed.

2

"You're real good," she said. "But I ain't thinkin' of any change. Uncle Pinker means well by me, and the work ain't too hard, 'cept come hayin' time, and along through the spring, sometimes, when I have to help in the gardin. I'm sure I'm obliged to *you!*" she added gratefully, with a shy, sweet look in her eyes that made Romulus feel as if the day had grown suddenly warm again.

"Well!" he said, with an effort, "I reely must be going, I suppose. I've had a good rest, and I must be getting on."

But Narcissa was not ready to have him go now. Her heart had been stirred by the unwonted kindness, the interest which this handsome stranger with the kind eyes had shown in her, Narcissa White, who was of no account to any one in the world. Her heart was stirred, and now she must show her gratitude in such simple wise as she could. She made him sit down at the table, and brought him doughnuts and milk, and the prettiest apples she could find in the cellar. In fear and trembling she took from the cupboard a tumbler of apple jelly, wondering as she did so what Uncle Pinker would say, and whether he would call it stealing. She had made the sweetmeat herself, and had earned the money to buy a half-dozen tumblers, by braiding rugs for Mrs. Parshley. She had picked the apples, too. Altogether, she thought she had a right to offer the jelly to the kind stranger.

He was delighted with his little feast, and pronounced the jelly the best he had ever tasted. She made it herself? he wanted to know! girls were smart on the road to Rome, he guessed. He drank her health from the brown mug, and again she apologized for not having a glass to give him. " There is good glasses," she said with a blush, " but Uncle Pinker keeps 'em locked up. I broke one when I first come here, two years ago, and he 's never let me touch one sence."

Romulus Patten muttered something in confidence to the brown mug, but Narcissa did not hear it. She was too happy to think that other people might consider Uncle Pinker a mean old curmudgeon. She felt a warmth about the heart, wholly strange to her starved and barren life. It had been dear and precious to dream, oh, yes! but here was reality. Here was some one like the people she dreamed about, only real flesh and blood, instead of shadows. He cared, this wonderful person, really cared, to be kind to her, to say pleasant words, and smile, and look at her with his bright, gentle eyes. And he was going to Rome! that was almost the best part of all, for now she could fancy him there, and would have some one to speak to, when she made her shadowy journeys to the Dream City.

She was hardly sorry when, the simple feast over, her new friend rose to go. It could not last forever, and Uncle Pinker would be waking up soon, and was apt to be "a little set," as she charitably expressed it, when he first woke. She made apologies for not having roused the old man, and was sure he would have been "real pleased" to see Mr. Patten, if it had been any other time of the day. She was a little startled when Romulus held out his hand at parting. She had an idea that people only shook hands at funerals; but she laid her little brown palm in the warm, strong one held out to her, and felt a cordial pressure that brought the tears to her eyes, — the sweet, forlorn gray eyes that never guessed at their own sweetness or sadness! Romulus Patten looked long into them before he let the little hand go.

"I sha' n't forget you, Miss White," he cried. "You may be sure of that; and I hope you won't forget me, either, for a spell. I may stop on my way back, if I don't have to go round another way when I leave Rome. I 'll try my best to fix it so as I can come back this way, and then — then perhaps you 'll let me call you Narcissa. Good-by — Narcissa!"

"Good-by!" echoed Narcissa; and then she stood on the doorstep and watched him, her new friend, the first friend she had ever had, as looking back often, and waving his hand once and twice in sign of farewell, he passed along down the road to Rome.

Part II.

WAKING.

"GOOD mornin', sir; can I sell you anything this mornin'?"

It was a strong, clear voice that broke rudely in upon Uncle Pinker's morning meditations as he sat in the doorway (the same setting that had framed Narcissa yesterday, but how different a picture!), smoking his short black pipe.

"Can I sell you anything?" repeated the voice, with an imperious intonation. Uncle Pinker looked up. The sound was a mere murmur in his ears; but when he saw the figure before him, he recognized it for one he had sometimes seen on the road, and knew instinctively what was wanted. "Ga-a-ah!" said Uncle Pinker.

This remark was a favorite one of the old gentleman's, and though no one knew its precise derivation, there was no doubt of its being the quintessence of scornful refusal. He used it constantly, but it never had such bitter force as when he was asked to spend money. "Ga-a-ah!" said Uncle Pinker again.

"What might you mean by that?" asked the newcomer, with some asperity. "That ain't no form of salutation ever I heard yet. Have n't you a civil tongue to use, old gentleman? You 're ancient enough to have learned manners, if you 'll excuse me sayin' so."

The old man snarled again. " I 'm stone deef!" he said. " I don't hear nothin' you say, nor yet I don't want to hear. You need n't waste no time, fur as I 'm concerned."

"Stone deef, be you?" returned the pedlar. " Well, that has its compensations, too. You would n't buy anything if you had the hearin' of ten, and now I can have the pleasure of tellin' you what I think of you. You skinny, starved old weasel, you 're about the wickedest-lookin' piece I ever set eyes on. Real old screw, you are, if ever I saw one. Pity your folks, if you 've got any; more likely you 've starved 'em all off, though, and are skeered of dyin' yourself, fear of havin' another funeral to pay for. The Lord leaves folks like you for a warnin' to others, understand? — set up, kind of, to show how ugly a critter can be when he tries. Oh, you need n't snarl at me. I 'm enjoyin' myself real well, I tell you. There 's other ways to have a good time besides sellin', if it is my trade. Guess I 'll set down a spell, uncle, sence you *are* so pressin'."

Uncle Pinker was almost foaming with rage by this time. He could hear no distinct words, but the insulting nature of the stranger's speech was evident from look and gesture. He was just wondering whether his strength would suffice to throw himself on the intruder, when a new figure appeared on the scene, — Narcissa, who had been busy in the back kitchen, and catching some high note of the stranger's scornful speech, now came hurrying out to see what was the matter.

She found Uncle Pinker quivering in his chair, his lean, veined hands clutching the arms, his little red eyes starting from his head with impotent fury; and sitting on the doorstep, looking up into his face with a smile of calm amusement, was the strangest figure Narcissa had ever seen.

A person of middle age, with strongly marked features, and a countenance of keen intelligence, but dressed in a singular manner. A suit of brown cloth, rather worn, but well-brushed and neat; loose trousers, and an odd, long-skirted coat, reaching to the knees, both coat and trousers trimmed with rows of narrow black-velvet ribbon. The person's hair was cropped short; the person's head was surmounted by a curious structure, half cap, half helmet, like that worn by Miss Deborah in " Cranford, " only of far humbler materials. Beside the person, on the doorstep, lay a bag, of the kind affected by pedlars, lank and shiny, and particularly unattractive in appearance.

Such was the individual at whom Narcissa White was now staring with eyes very wide open, her stare being returned by a quizzical gaze, half smiling, and wholly shrewd and observant.

"Mornin', young lady," said the strong, clear voice.

"Wonderin' what I be, are ye? fish or flesh, or red
herrin', or what, hey? Well, I'll put you out of your
misery. I'm a woman, that's what I am; the folks
calls me Bloomer Joe. Now, then, do you want to
buy anything of me?"

Here her tone changed, and her voice rose and fell
in a kind of chant, dwelling with dramatic emphasis
on a telling phrase here and there.

"Buy any lace, threads, or needles, pins — *or* — es-
sences? Here's a looking-glass to see your face in —
prettiest face I've seen along the road! (I tell that to
every girl I see, and most of 'em believe it; but you
ain't that kind, so you shall have the joke instead.)
Real celluloid ivory combs, fit for the President's wife,
sure enough. Gold beads, stockin'-supporters, teeth-
brushes, — *and* — stickin'-plaster."

Here she dropped back into a conversational tone,
opening her bag as she did so, and drawing forth some
of its treasures.

"Just look at this lace, young lady! strong enough
to hang yourself with, if you was feelin' that way, or
to hang the old gentleman here, if you was feelin'
another. I know which way I'd feel, quick enough.
Not your father, is he?" she added, seeing a look of
distress in Narcissa's eyes.

"Oh, no," said Narcissa, speaking for the first time.
"But — he's my uncle, — at least, my father's uncle;
and I — guess you'd better not talk so, please."

" All right," said the stranger. " I won't, not if it is any trouble to you. It would be meat and potatoes and apple-pie for me, if he was my uncle, to hear him get his rights for once in a way; but I see you 're one of the soft-hearted ones. Want any salve? Here 's a kind that will cure corns, bunions, rheumatism, croup, sore-throat, backache, horse-ail, and colic; cure most anything except a broken heart, and won't do a mite of harm to that. But you don't need any salve, and the old gentleman, he 's past it. Well, then, here 's ribbons, all colors of the rainbow, — red, yeller, blue, see? handsome they are, and cheap as good counsel. Aha! you 'd like to see them, hey?"

Narcissa had indeed changed color at sight of the bright ribbons, and she now gave an anxious glance at Uncle Pinker, who was still fuming and snorting in his chair.

"You, Narcissy White, send this critter away, can't ye?" he snarled; "or else go into the house yourself, and go to work, not stand foolin' here, with the work all on the floor. Go 'long, d' ye hear? This woman, or feller, or whatever she calls herself, can talk till she 's hoarse; she won't hurt me, nor she won't get nothin' out of me."

"Could I get a drink of water, do you s'pose?" the pedlar asked quietly, paying no attention to the angry old man. "Need n't trouble to bring it out; I 'll go right into the house with you, if you 've no objections."

She followed Narcissa into the house before the latter could make any remonstrance, and shut the door after her.

"He don't reelly disturb me," she said, "not a mite; but we can trade better in here. Let me try some of the ribbons on your hair. I don't often see such hair as this on my tramps, and that's no compliment, but the plain truth."

"Oh!" cried Narcissa, in distress. "You're real kind, but please don't. I have n't got any money to buy things with, and I could n't take your time for nothing. They are handsome, ain't they? Oh, that yellow is just elegant, is n't it? It's like the buttons; I mean like the tansy blossoms. I thank you for showin' them to me, I'm sure, but it ain't any use for you to."

"Don't he pay you for workin' here?" asked the pedlar, with a sharp glance.

"Yes, he does pay me," Narcissa answered, — "a dollar and a half a week. But — but I don't get it very reg'lar, sometimes, and I'm saving up to buy me a dress. I need one bad, to wear to meetin'."

The pedlar frowned. It was against her principles to leave any house where she knew there was money, without selling at least a box of salve; but this seemed a hard case.

"A dollar and a half a week!" she muttered scornfully. "The old caraway seed! he'd better go and live in Rome, and be done with it. He'll find plenty of company there."

Narcissa looked up with wide-open eyes.

"Why do you say that?" she asked.

"Because Rome is the skinniest place on this round earth," was the reply; "and I think 't would suit your uncle down to the ground."

Still the girl gazed. "I guess you 're mistaken," she said quietly. "I guess you never was there, was you?"

"Never till yesterday," replied the woman, "and never want to be there again. You see, this is n't my own country at all, as you may say. I belong in another part of the State, and most generally keep to my own beat, havin' my regular customers, understand? and goin' round amongst 'em. But oncet in a while the fancy takes me to roam a little, and see other parts; and so I come round through Damascus and Solon, and passed through Rome yesterday."

"Oh!" cried Narcissa, breathlessly. "You did? do tell me! and was n't it elegant? I don't see how you could come away. Did you walk about, and see all them handsome buildings? and did you see the folks?"

The pedlar gazed at her in wonder. The girl's eyes were like stars, her whole face alight with enthusiasm. What did it mean?

"Handsome buildin's?" she repeated. "In Rome? I 'll tell you what I saw, child, and then you 'll know. I saw the forlornest place on this earth, I don't care where the next may be. I saw rocks and turkeys, and turkeys and rocks. The street (if you can call it a street; 't would be called a hog-wallow, down where I come from) is solid rock where it ain't mud, and solid mud where it ain't rock. There 's a house here and a house there, and they all look as if they was tryin' to get away from each other, but did n't darse to move for fear of fallin' down.

"The folks I saw were as lean as their own turkeys, and I can't say no further than that. I tried to sell 'em some of my salve; told 'em 't would heal the skin where 't was broke with the bones comin' through, but they was past jokin' with.

"I tell you, child, Rome is the.— Why, what 's the matter?" The good woman stopped suddenly, for Narcissa was trembling all over, and her face shone white in the dim, half-lighted room.

"I — I don't understand you!" she cried wildly. "There 's some mistake ; you went to the wrong place, and never saw Rome at all. Look here!" and she led the way swiftly across the hall, into the other room, the room into which she had taken Romulus Patten the day before. She almost ran up to the picture, and motioned the pedlar, with an imperious gesture, strange in so gentle a creature, to look at it. "That is Rome!" cried Narcissa. "You went to the wrong place, I tell you. This — this is Rome!"

The woman drew out a pair of spectacles, and fitted

them on her nose with exasperating deliberation. She took a long look at the picture, and then turned to the trembling girl, with a kind light of pity in her eyes struggling with amusement.

" You poor — deluded — child ! " she said at length. " Who ever told you that was Rome, I should like to know ? "

" But it says so ! " cried Narcissa. " Can't you read ? ' ROME.' There it is, in plain letters ; and I — don't — " she wanted to say " I don't believe you ! " but the blue eyes that met hers steadily showed nothing but truth and kindness.

" So it is Rome, dear ! " said the pedlar, speaking now very gently. " But it's ancient Rome, over in Europe ; Italy, they call the country. Where the ancient Romans lived; don't you know ? Julius Cæsar, and all those fellers who cut up such didoes, hundreds of years ago ? Don't tell me you never went to school, nor learned any history."

" I — I went for a spell ! " Narcissa faltered. " I had to leave when I was fourteen, because I was wanted to home, and we had n't only got to the Battle of Lexington in history. I did hope to learn about the Revolution, to home, but father's wife did n't think much of readin', and she burned up the book."

There was a silence, and then the good-natured pedlar began fumbling in her bag.

"It's a livin' shame!" she cried indignantly.
"Here — no, it ain't, neither. Well! I did think,
much as could be, that I had two or three little books
here, and I should have been pleased to give you one,
dear, just for keeps, you know. But they don't seem
to be here. Well, never mind! I was goin' to ask if
you wouldn't like this piece of yeller ribbon you
seemed to take to. It's a real good piece, and I should
be pleased — I declare, child, I do feel bad to have
spoiled your pretty notion of Rome. I s'pose you
thought likely you'd go there some day, hey? well,
well! sit down, and let me put this ribbon on your
hair. You no need to be scairt of me. I act kind o'
wild sometimes, like I did with your uncle, but it's four
parts fun. I'm well known up our way, and anybody 'll
tell you I come of good stock, if I am crazy enough to
wear sensible clothes, that don't hender me walkin'
nor settin'. Mis' Transom, my name is. And he
called you Narcissy, did n't he? Why, I had a cousin
once, name of Narcissy; it's not a common name
either, and I allers thought it was real pretty. Set
down here, dear, and let's talk a spell."

Thus the kind woman rattled on, watching the
girl keenly the while. She was making time for
her, giving her a chance to recover from what was
evidently a heavy blow.

But Narcissa scarcely heard her. She was dazed;
her dream was shattered, her glorious city laid in

ruins, the beauty and romance of her whole life dashed away, as a rude touch dashes the dew from the morning grass.

As she sat, trying to realize it, trying to think that it really was not so much, that there would be other pleasant things, perhaps, to fill the barren working days, and gild the grayness of the long lonely Sabbaths, — as she sat thus, a new thought flashed into her mind, piercing like the thrust of a sword.

Her friend, Romulus Patten! She had sent him off on a false scent, had lied to him about the place, the city — she could hardly bear even to think of its dishonored name now. He had gone there, thinking to find what she had told him about, — the stately houses, the arches, the soft sunshine gilding all. What would he think of her when he found it was all a cheat, a lie? He had been kind to her, had seemed to care about her as nobody had ever done in her forlorn young life; and this was how she had repaid him!

She started up, shrinking as if from some cruel sting. "I must go and tell him!" she cried. "I lied to him, though I did n't know it was a lie. I must go and find him, and tell him I did n't mean to."

"Tell who?" cried the pedlar, catching her by the arm. "What is it troubles you so, Narcissy? Who did you lie to, I should like to know? Don't believe she could tell a decent lie if 't was to save her own soul," she added to herself.

But Narcissa did not heed her.

She had taken down her sunbonnet from a nail, and was tying it under her chin with trembling fingers, with a feverish haste that took no note of anything.

"Where are you going?" cried Mrs. Transom, now beginning to be frightened at the girl's distracted looks. "You're never going out of the house feeling like this? You'll have a fit of sickness, sure as you're alive, and then where'll you be? and 't is all foolishness, too, I'll be bound. I can't understand a word you say. And there's a storm coming up, too. I see it as I was coming along, and was reckoning on finding shelter here when I fust stopped to speak to the old gentleman. There, hear the thunder this very minute! Narcissy! Why, good land of deliverance, she's gone!"

The storm came on very suddenly, — first, a low bank of cloud heaving in sight on the western horizon, long and misshapen, like the back of a kraken; then the whole monster revealed, rising across the sky, tossing monstrous arms about, showing ugly tints of yellow, ugly depths of purple and black.

There was no lightning at first, only low mutterings of thunder, and every now and then a pale lifting of the darkness, as if the monster were opening his cavernous jaws, showing glimpses of dim horror within.

Then, of a sudden, with no note of warning, the whole sky sprang into flame, the whole air was a roar and a bellow, deafening the ears, stunning the senses, — and the storm broke over the road to Rome.

The rain struck aslant, driving a spray before it, as of a mountain stream. In five minutes no road was to be seen, — only a long stretch of brown water, hissing and writhing under the scourge of the rain and wind. A horse came plodding carefully along, crouching together as well as he could, picking his way through the water. The two men in the buggy behind him were crouching, too, and trying to hide behind the rubber boot. It was some comfort to think that they were trying to keep dry, though both knew that they were already drenched to the skin.

"It's lucky for me that I met you," said the younger of the two, shaking himself, and sending a shower of spray in all directions.

"P'r'aps 't is just as well," replied the other man, with a chuckle. "You'd hardly have known yourself from a muskrat by this time, if you'd had to foot it from Rome here. Been stoppin' there?"

"Stopping as long as I cared to," said the youth, who was no other than our friend Romulus Patten. "I got there last night, and was good and ready to come away this morning. I'm travelling for Brown's Nurseries, and there don't seem to be any call for any of our goods in Rome. Stone-crop's the only plant they raise much of, I guess."

3

"Well, that's so," said the elder man. "That's so,
every time. I never knew but one man that could
make anything grow in Rome, and he carted all the
dirt three miles, over from North Podley, before he
could make a seed grow. Yes, sir, he did so. Mighty
poor country up that way. Some say the Rome folks
don't see any garden-truck from year's end to year's
end, and that if you ask a Rome girl to cook you up a
mess of string beans, she takes the store beans and
runs 'em on a string, and boils 'em that way; but I
dono. I'm from Vi-enny way myself."

"My gracious! what's that?"

The whole world had turned to livid white for a
moment, dazzling and blinding them; but still they
had seen something on the road, something like a hu-
man form, torn and buffeted by the wind and the
furious rain, but staggering on towards them with
uncertain steps.

"My God! it's a woman!" cried Romulus Patten.
"Stop your horse, and let me get out. A woman, alone
in this storm!"

He sprang to the ground, and holding his arm before
his face to keep off the blinding rain, made his way
towards the forlorn figure splashing through the water,
now ankle deep in the road, stumbling, often on the
point of falling.

"Hold up, lady!" he called out, in his cheery voice.
"There's friends here! Hold up just a minute!"

At the sound of his voice the woman stopped and seemed to shudder and clasp her hands. "I never meant it!" she cried out wildly. "I can't see you, I'm most blind, but I know your voice. I never meant to lie to you about Rome. I — thought — 't was all true; and when I found out, I — came — to tell you. I never meant to send you there on a lie."

"Narcissa!" cried Romulus Patten. "Oh, Lord! Oh, you poor little thing! and you thought I did n't know? I'd ought to be shot, that's what I ought to be. Here, you poor little thing, let me take your hands! They're like wet ice, and you're shivering all over. Oh, dear me! come with me, and get right into this buggy out of the rain. Oh, Lord! and I let you go on thinking I did n't know!"

Half leading, half carrying her, he made his way to the buggy, and then fairly lifted her in his strong young arms to lay her on the seat; but here an obstacle was interposed in the shape of another arm as strong as his, and a good deal bigger. "Easy, there!" said the owner of the buggy. "Seems to me you're makin' yourself rather too free, young feller. Do you think I'm goin' to have that gal brought in here, runnin' all the rivers of Babylon? Who in Jerusalem is she, anyway? Some of your folks?"

Romulus Patten's face was streaming with cold rain, but he flushed as if a flame had swept over him.

"She's the young lady I'm going to marry," he said.

"Will you take her in, or shall I carry her home this way?"

"Now you're talking!" the stranger said, removing his arm and making way. "Why did n't you speak up before, sonny? Here, give me a holt of her!" He lifted Narcissa gently into the buggy, and drew her close to his side, laying her head well up on his shoulder so that she could breathe easily. "Family man," he explained. "Gals of my own. Now you reach under the seat there, and bring out a shawl you'll find."

Romulus obeyed, and half angry, half pleased, watched the stranger as he deftly wrapped the shawl round the fainting girl, and put her dripping hair tenderly off her face.

"Allers take a shawl along," he explained further. "Wife enjoys poor health, and have to be ready for a change of wind. Comes in handy, don't it? Now get in, young feller, and tell me where to drive to. You need n't look down in the mouth, either, 'cause you don't know everything in creation yet. Time enough to learn, and you're likely to learn easy, I should say.

"And you rest comfortable, my dear," he added, speaking to Narcissa as if she were a small child. "Here's your friend alongside of you, and you're just as safe as you would be in the best stuffed chair in the settin'-room at home. Fetch your breath, like a good girl, and try to look about you."

But Narcissa heard never a word, for she had fainted.

An hour later, Romulus Patten and Mrs. Transom were sitting by Narcissa's bedside, watching her. She had fallen into a deep, childlike sleep, and their low voices did not disturb her.

"The old gentleman was so mad he was all cheesed up," the pedlar was saying. "There! I was fairly sorry for him, old weasel as he is; so I let him go on for a spell, till he was clean tuckered out, and then I e'en took him up and put him to bed, same as if he was a child. Glad enough he was to get there too, if he was mad. Then I took and made him some warm drink, and gave him to understand I'd stay by till Narcissy come back, and here I be. And now, young man," she added, fixing her keen blue eyes on Romulus's face, "I've got a word to say to you. You let fall something when you was bringin' this child in — I won't say that I was n't mighty glad to see her, and you, too, — but you let on something about keepin' company with her. Now, I want to know right here, what you meant, and who you are, and all about it. Oh, you may look at my pants much as you're a mind to. I come of good folks, and I dress as seems fit to me, and I don't care in any way, shape, or manner what folks say or think. I've been snoopin' round some, since I put that old man to bed, and I found the family Bible; and this child is the lawful

daughter of my cousin, Narcissy Merrill, that I have n't
heard of this twenty years. Bein' so, I 'm goin' to
stand by her, as is right and proper; so, now I 'll hear
what you 've got to say. I 've as good a right to do for
her as that old skimp-jack in there, if he *is* her father's
uncle."

Romulus Patten spoke out frankly. He had " taken
to " Narcissa from the first moment he saw her. When
was that? Well, it was n't long ago, it was true. It
was only yesterday; but he was n't one to change,
and he had never seen a girl yet that he would look
twice at. And when she came, in all that awful storm,
just to tell him, — here the young man choked a little,
and the woman liked him the better for it, — he made
up his mind then, he went on, all in a minute, that she
should be his wife; and she should, if so be she was
willing. He would go back to the place and see if he
could get a job in the garden; he might have had one
now, but he was some tired and had thought it would
rest him to travel a spell. He would quit travelling
now, and had little doubt that he could have a good
place.

He knew of a pleasant rent — in that part of the
country a hired tenement is known as a " rent "— with
four rooms, that belonged to a friend of his, and he
could get that, he guessed. In short, the sooner Narcissa got away from Uncle Pinker the better, in his
opinion, and he was ready to take her, the first day she

would go. That was all he had to say for himself; but
he presumed Mr. Brown would give him a character if
he was asked. He had worked for Browns three years,
and had no reason to think they were n't satisfied
with him.

When Romulus had finished his little speech, which
left him flushed and tremulous, yet with a brave light
in his eyes, and a tender look as he glanced towards his
love where she lay sleeping quietly, Mrs. Transom
gazed at him for a while in silence; then she held out
her hand and grasped his heartily.

"I guess you 'll do," she said. "I guess you 're the
right sort. Now, I 'll tell you what. You go along
and get your place, and see about your rent. Don't
engage it, but get the refusal of it, if it belongs to a
friend, as you say. Then you come back here and find
your girl all well and peart again, and you say your
say, and let her say hers. You don't want to take
advantage of her being sick and weakly now — now,
you no need to flare up! I say you don't want to, and
I mean it. You 'll need a box of my salve, if you 're
so thin-skinned as all that comes to.

"You go along, I say, and when you come back,
come over to my place, Tupham Corner, third house
from the cross-road, white house with a yeller door.
Everybody knows Mis' Transom's house. You 'll find
your gal there, and you 'll marry her there, with her
mother's cousin to stand up with her. There, don't

be scairt! Pity some gals have n't got the trick of
blushin' as you have, young man.   I 've got as good a
black silk as any in Tupham or Cyrus, and nobody's
goin' to say 'Bloomer Joe' round where my own folks
live, you 'd better believe.   What say?   Like my idee,
or have you got a better one yourself?"

"You 're real good!" Romulus cried.   "Poor little
Narcissa!   It does seem as if she had found all her
friends at once, and she never having any in her life
before, as you may say.   I tell you, Mis' Transom, I 'll
treat her as well as I know how.   If she was a queen,
she should n't have any more care than what I 'll give
her.   I — I think a sight of her!" he added simply.
"Seems as if she always belonged to me, somehow."

"That 's right!" said Mrs. Transom, who was as
romantic as any lady in silk and satin.   "That 's right,
young man.   We 'll get her away from this old rat-
hole, and then I guess it 'll be a good while before
either you or I travels this way again, hey?"

"I don't know as I have anything to say against the
country," said Romulus Patten, with another loving
look at the sleeper.   "It is n't exactly the place to sell
trees, but yet there 's good things to be found on this
road, — the road to Rome."

IN VERONA.

IN VERONA.

FIRST of all, let me correct the mistaken impression that my title cannot fail to make upon the patient reader. On reading the words, "In Verona," his mind instantly conjures up a vision of white palaces; of narrow streets across which the tall houses nod at each other, hinting at the mysteries they dare not reveal; of ancient fountains, embowered in myrtle and laurel; finally, of Juliet's tomb, and a thousand memories of the immortal lovers.

All this is natural, but it will not do. Here in Verona are no fountains, but half a dozen old well-sweeps, and all the rest cucumber-wood pumps; no palaces, but neat white houses with green blinds, and flowers in their front-yards; no laurel, but good honest sunflowers instead; finally, no tomb of Juliet, for our Juliet did not die; briefly, and to have done with mystery, our Verona is in the State of Maine.

I have often wondered what manner of men they were, who named the towns in the good old State. Lyceum teachers for the most part, one would think, —

men who had read books, and whose hearts yearned
for the historic glories of the old world, glories which
their narrow lives might never see. So, disagreeing
with this same Juliet in the matter of names, they did
what they could, and not being able to go to Europe,
did their best to bring Europe over into their own new
country. So we have here in Maine Rome and Paris,
Palermo and Vi-enny (miscalled " Vienna " by pedants,
and those thinking themselves better than other people), Berlin Falls and South China, — in fact, half the
continent to choose from, all in our own door-yard, as
it were.

You may not find Verona on the county-map; you
certainly will not see it as you flash by on the Maine
Central Railway, on your way to Bar Harbor. But if
you travel for a certain length of time on a certain quiet
road, grass-grown for the most part, and with only a few
straggling cottages dotting it here and there, — if, as I
say, you travel long enough, and do not get out of
patience and turn back towards Vi-enny, you will come
suddenly round a bend of the road, and there will be
Verona before you, all white and smiling, tucked away
under the great hill-shoulder that curls lovingly round
it. The cleanest, freshest, sleepiest little New England
village! No myrtle, no laurel, not the faintest suggestion of a fountain! Yet here lived and loved, not so
very long ago, Romeo and Juliet.

They were simple young people; they did not even

know their own names, for Juliet answered to the name of Betsy Garlick, while Romeo was known only as Bije Green; and they worked for the Bute girls.

It is well known that the Bute girls — who might better be spoken of, if the custom of the country allowed it, as the Misses Bute — did not speak to each other. They lived in two white cottages, side by side, on the Indiana road; and though they could not avoid seeing each other every day, no communication had taken place between them since the time of their mother's death, some ten years ago. Old Mrs. Bute had been partly responsible, all the neighbors thought, for this unfortunate state of things. She was a masterful woman, and never allowed her daughters to call their souls their own, even when they were middle-aged women. Though both gifted with strong wills, they lived in absolute subjection to the small withered autocrat who hardly ever stirred from her armchair in the chimney-corner.

She persisted in treating her daughters, either of whom could have picked her up with one hand and set her on the mantelpiece, as if they were little children; and they accepted the position with meekness.

It was even said that when Mrs. Bute felt called on to die, as we say in Verona, she insisted on having her daughters' mourning made and tried on in her presence, that she might be sure of its being respectable, and fitting properly. " Neither one of you has sense to know when a gown wrinkles in the back," she said. " I couldn't lay easy in my grave, and you going round all hitched up between the shoulders."

So the village dressmaker cut the clothes (black stuff dresses, and black cambric pelisses lined with flannel), and came in fear and trembling to try them on. It must have been a grim scene: the two gaunt, middle-aged women standing meekly before the bed, turning this way and that at command; the dying woman issuing, in halting whispers, her directions for "seam and gusset and band," while death had her by the throat, fitting her for the straight white garment which was making in the next room. Not till she had seen her daughters arrayed in the completed costumes, with bonnet and veil to match, would Eliza Bute turn her face to the wall and go, feeling that she had done her duty.

Perhaps it was hardly to be wondered at, if, so soon as the iron grasp was loosened which had held them all their days, the two women went to the other extreme, and could brook no suggestion of authority from any one, least of all from each other. Perhaps each was sure that Mother (awful shade, still hovering on the borders of their life!) would be of her way of thinking; however it was, the two sisters quarrelled the day after the funeral. The will was read, and it was found that the property was to be evenly divided between them. Evenly divided! It was a dangerous phrase. Miss Duty had her idea of what "even" meant, and Miss Resigned Elizabeth had hers; and neither was likely to give up to the other. They listened in grim silence as the lawyer read the will; and each decided that she knew what Mother meant, and 't was n't likely the other did.

The strife that followed was grim, though not loud. No wrangling was heard; no neighbor was called in to keep the peace; but after three days, Miss Resigned Elizabeth sent for a man and a wheelbarrow, and removed with all her goods and chattels to the house next door, which was hers by right of inheritance from her grandmother.

A neighbor calling on Miss Duty the day after. the separation, found her in the spare chamber, seated before the bed, on which were spread out divers articles of the personal property which had been her mother's. There was one black lace mitt, six white stockings and six gray ones, half of an embroidered apron, ditto of a nankeen waistcoat in which Father Bute had been married; item, one infant's sock; item, three left-hand shoes. Here, on what was evidently the half of a green veil, lay a slender store of trinkets: one mosaic earring, one garnet one, half of a string of gold beads, and — piteous sight! — half of a hair bracelet, its strands, roughly cut, already half unbraided, and sticking out in silent protest against the inhuman treatment they had received.

The neighbor broke out into indignant inquiry, but was quickly silenced. Miss Duty was satisfied, and so was her sister; that being so, she did n't know that the neighbors had any call to be distressed. Good Mrs. Dill went home in high indignation, and before night all Verona knew how "ridiklous" the Bute girls had behaved, and joined with Mrs. Dill in thinking that Old Ma'am Bute had better have left them a "gardeen," if that was all they knew about how to treat good stuff, as had cost more money than ever they were likely to earn.

When Bije Green came to work for Miss Duty Bute, he knew nothing of the feud between the two houses. He was not a Veronese, but came from that mysterious region known as "out back," meaning the remote country. When, working in the garden, he saw on the other side of the fence an old woman (any person above thirty was old to Bije) who looked almost exactly like the old woman who had hired him, it seemed the proper thing to say "hullo!" to her, that being the one form of salutation known to Bije; but instead of an answering "hullo!" he met a stony stare, which sent him back in confusion to his potatoes. "She's deef!" said Bije to himself, charitably. "And my old woman 's nigh about dumb, — quite an asylum between 'em." And he whistled "Old Dog Tray" till Miss Duty came and told him to stop that racket!

Poor Bije! he found life dull, at first, on the Indiana

road. He was shy, and not one to make acquaintances easily, even if Miss Duty had approved of his running down to the village, which she did not. But he was used to cheerful conversation at home, and felt the need of it strongly here. His innocent attempts at entertaining Miss Duty were generally met with a "H'm!" which did not encourage further remarks. "Nice day!" he would say in a conciliating manner, when he brought in the wood in the early morning. "H'm!" Miss Duty would reply, with a frosty glance in his direction.

"Havin' nice weather right along!"

If he met with any reply to this suggestion, it would be a "H'm!" even more forbidding; while a third remark, if he ever ventured on one, would be answered by swift dismissal to the woodshed, with the admonition not to be "gormin' round here, with all the work to do."

These things being so, Bije was sad at heart, and pined for a certain corner of the fence at home, and his sister Delilah leaning over it, talking while he hoed. Delilah was only a girl, but she could be some company; and what was the use of having a tongue, if you never used it, 'cept just to jaw people? Jawing never did no good that he could make out, though he did n't know but he'd ruther be jawed than hear nothing at all from get up to go to bed.

Such thoughts as these were in Bije's mind one

4

morning, as he wrestled with the witch-grass on the strip of green near the fence which divided Miss Duty's lot from her sister's. He did not like witch-grass; he never could see the use of the pesky stuff. Delilah was always saying that there was use for everything; Bije wished she were here, to tell him the use of witch-grass. He guessed — At this moment the tail of his eye caught a flutter, as of a petticoat, beyond the dividing fence. Now Miss Resigned Elizabeth's petticoats never fluttered; they were not full enough. Bije looked up, and saw — a girl.

She was standing in the porch, polishing the milk-pails. She had curly, fair hair, which she kept shaking back out of her eyes, — blue eyes, as bright as the little pond at home, when the sun shone on it in the morning. The red-and-white of her cheeks was so pure and clear, that Bije thought at once of a snow-apple; and his hand made an instinctive movement towards his pocket, though it was not near the time for "snows." There was not much wind, and yet this girl's things seemed "all of a flutter;" her pink calico gown, her blue-checked apron, her flying curls, — all were full of life and dancing motion. The milk-pails twinkled in the morning sun, catching fresh gleams as she turned them this way and that. They were not common milk-pails, it appeared, but pure silver, or they could not twinkle so. Also, the sun was brighter than usual. Bije stood gazing, with no knowledge that his mouth was open and his brown eyes staring in a very rude way. The witch-grass took breath, and rested from the fierce assaults of the hoe. Bije knew nothing of witch-grass. He had never heard of such a thing. There were only two things in the whole world, so far as he knew : a milk-pail and Betsy Garlick.

When Betsy looked up, as of course she did in a moment, she saw no fairy vision, but only a boy : a brown boy, in brown overalls, with his mouth open, staring as if he had never seen a girl in his life before. Betsy had seen plenty of boys, and she was not in the least afraid of them ; so she returned Bije's stare with a calm survey which took him all in, from his conscious head to his awkward heels, and then, with a toss of her curls and a click of pails, disappeared into the house.

All that day, Bije went about in a dream. When Miss Duty asked him what he had been doing all the morning, he answered " Milk-pails ; " and when she asked what they used to keep off potato-bugs out his way, he could only say " Pink calico." At this atrocious statement, Miss Duty turned sharply on him. " Bijah Green," she said, " if you are goin' loony, I 'll thank you to take yourself off home. I don't want no naturals round here, so now you know."

Bije was terribly frightened at this. Yesterday it would have been rather a good joke to be discharged by the old lady, and go home to the farm with a month's wages in his pocket; to-day, it seemed the most dreadful calamity that could happen to him; and he hastened to give such an eloquent description of the potato-bug war, as carried on in West Athens (pronounced Aythens) that Miss Duty was mollified, and reckoned she must try paris green herself. When evening came, Bije went early for his cow, and milked that good beast with undue haste and trepidation. Then, having carried the brimming pails into the kitchen, he returned to the shed, and looked about him with gleaming eyes. Yes, there it was! the knot-hole that he had found the other day, when he was brushing down the cobwebs, — just opposite the back-porch of the house across the way. She would be coming out again in a minute; it was n't likely that she had done milking yet. He drew up a broken stool, and seating himself on it, flattened his face against the rough boards of the shed, and waited. The door of the house across the way opened, and Miss Resigned Elizabeth came slowly out. She was younger than Miss Duty, but she looked older, being near-sighted, and walking with a stoop and a shuffle. She was rather good-looking, with soft brown hair, and a little autumnal red in her thin cheeks; but to Bije's distorted vision, she seemed the most horrible old hag that had ever darkened the earth. Her scant gray skirt (made out of her half of a dress of Mother Bute's, who wore her skirts full), her neck-handkerchief, her

carpet slippers, all were an offence to him; and he
could hardly resist the impulse to call out to her to
take herself out of his field of vision, and leave it clear
for the desired one. The dreadful old woman! how she
stood round, as if folks wanted to see her, instead of
wishing she was in Jericho. She was actually sitting
down, taking out her old knitting! Such things ought
not to be allowed. There ought to be a law against
ugly women — Hark! what was that? Miss Resigned
Elizabeth was calling to somebody, — to somebody in
the house. "Betsy! Betsy Garlick! come out here,
will you?"

Why, this was not such a horrid old lady after all.
Now he thought of it, she was rather nice-looking, for
an old one. The door was opening, opening wider.
There she came with her pails. The wonderful girl!
not flashing and sparkling, as in the morning light,
but with the softness of twilight in her eyes and her
lovely waving hair. What was it the other lad said,
over there in the old Verona, at a minute like this?

> "Oh, she doth teach the torches to burn bright!
> Her beauty hangs upon the cheek of night
> Like a rich jewel in an Ethiop's ear!"

and so on, in his glowing, tropical way. But Bije
could not say anything of that sort. His heart was as
high as Romeo's, and seemed to be beating in his
throat, as he gazed at the fair vision; but he knew
nothing of language, and if he had tried to put his

thoughts into words, he would only have said : " Ain't
she slick ! " A most un-Shakespearian Bije ! an ordinary, good country-boy ! But no fiery gallant of them
all was ever thrilled with purer fire than burned now
in his veins. He wanted to do something, something
wonderful, for this girl. What did all those fellers
do, in the story-books Delilah was everlastingly reading ? He wished he had read some of the stories,
instead of laughing at them for girl's fool-talk. She
was smiling now ; did anybody ever smile like that
before ? Of course not ! He wished he were Miss
Resigned Elizabeth, to be smiled at in that way ; he
wondered what it felt like. But no ! the poor old
lady was deef ! (she was not in the least deaf, be it
said, by the way). Deef, and that girl talking to her !
Poor old lady ! It was a dreadful thing to be deef.

And so on, and so on : Ossa on Pelion of rapture
and young delight and wonder, when suddenly a heavy
hand was laid on his shoulder. The boy started as if
he had been shot. Miss Duty Bute whirled him
round, away from the opening into Paradise, — I
should say the knot-hole, — and stooping down,
applied her eye to the aperture.

The little scene on the porch of the opposite house
had no special charm for Miss Duty : she only saw her
sister, Resigned Eliz, as she had called her in former
days, and her hired girl. The butcher had told her
that Resigned Eliz had hired a girl ; also, she, Miss

Duty, had rheumatism in her joints, which made stooping painful to her. Therefore, when she straightened her poor back, and turned once more upon the trembling Bije, her mood was none of the softest. Briefly, he was told that if ever she caught him spying upon the other house, whensoever or howsoever, he would pack off that moment of time. He had no more to do with the other house than he had with the Plagues of Egypt, she'd have him to know; and when she wanted spying done, she could do it herself, without hiring no shif'less, long-legged, trifling boys to do it for her. Finally, was she to have any kindling-wood split that night, or was she not?

This was very dreadful, and for some days Bije hardly dared to look over the fence, much less to loiter in the shed for an instant. But what says the old song, the Lover's song, that perhaps (who knows?) may have been sung in the streets when Will Shakespeare was a little naughty boy?

> "Over the mountain,
>   And over the waves;
> Under the fountains,
>   And under the graves;
> Under floods that are deepest,
>   Which Neptune obey,
> Over rocks that are steepest,
>   Love will find out the way."

This being so, what could two elderly ladies, who seldom stirred from their own door-yards, save to go to meeting — what were they to do against the all-conquering little god, or against Abijah Green, his soldier and slave? Bije found out the way, unconscious of any fluttering wings about him, any mischievous, rosy imp with bow and arrow.

A posy laid on the fence; then an apple, polished on the coat-sleeve till it shone again; then two more apples and a posy beside them, to show that there could be no mistake about it.

Betsy was only eighteen, and if life was dull at Miss Duty's, it was not exciting at Miss Resigned Elizabeth's. She, too, had been cautioned to have nothing to do with "that bold-lookin' boy over t' the other house!" But Betsy did not think the boy was bold-looking. Anyhow, she hoped (but her hopes were not expressed aloud) she had manners enough to say thank you, when any one was pretty-behaved. So she said thank you, first with her eyes (because Miss Resigned Elizabeth was close by, watering the flower-beds), then with her lips; and it became evident to Bije that she had the sweetest voice that ever was heard in the world. The flowers were real pretty! Betsy thought a sight o' flowers. They had lots of pansies to home, and she did miss 'em, so these seemed real homelike. Did Mr. — well, there! some might think 't was queer for her to be talkin' to him, and never knowin' what his name was! Bijah Green? Betsy wanted to know! Why, she had an uncle named

Green, over to South Beulah. Not her own uncle — he married her aunt Phrony; real nice man, he was. She wondered if he was any relation. But what she was goin' to say? She did n't suppose Mr. Green cared for southernwood. There was a great root of it round by the back-door here; 't was dretful sweet, and she had to set it over, Miss Bute said. He could have a piece off the root, just as well as not; only she did n't s'pose he cared for such common doin's as southernwood.

It appeared that southernwood had been Mr. Green's favorite plant from his cradle, as one might say. If there was one thing he did hanker after, it was southernwood; but he could n't see her grubbin' up things that way. If he knew where the bush was, he could get it himself, just as easy —

Betsy would not hear of that! Besides, *she* was dretful pernickety about folks comin' into the yard. There! Betsy did n't know what she 'd say this minute, if she was to see her talkin' to him; but for her, Betsy's, part, she had allers been brought up to be neighborly. Bije chimed in eagerly. 'T was dretful lonesome, specially come evenin's. To see her ("her" in this case meant Miss Duty) settin' there, knittin' for dear life, and never a word to say to any one — 't was enough to make any one feel homesick. Not but what she was good, in her way, only 't was a tormentin', up-stiff kind o' way. Drivin' the cow, too! It did seem as though he should fly, sometimes, drivin'

that critter all alone from pasture. His sister allers
went with him, to home; he s'posed that's why it
seemed so lonesome now. Where did *she* (oh, New
England! oh, poor little hard-worked pronouns! this
"she" was Miss Resigned Elizabeth), — where did she
keep her cow? Seem's though —

Seems, Bijah? Nay, it is!

What are cows and country roads made for, I should
like to know, save for the pleasure of youths and
maidens? Miss Duty's cow was kept in the humplety
field, as the children called it, a mile and more from
Cuttyhunk, the pasture where Miss Resigned Elizabeth's good Brindle spent her peaceful days; yet it was
strange to see the intimacy that sprung up between
these two creatures in the next few weeks.

At a certain turn of the road, Brindle would stop
and fall to cropping the grass by the road-side, swing-
ing her body about and switching the flies off com-
fortably; while her driver, loitering a few steps behind,
pulled the early golden-rod or plaited sweet rushes
together, apparently absorbed in her task, and only
from time to time casting shy glances down the other
road, which led off, over hill and dale, to Cuttyhunk.
But, by-and-by, down this other road would come
another cow, — not a happy, leisurely cow like Brindle,
but a breathless and much-tormented beast who had
been hurried out of all nature ever since she left the
pasture, absolutely goaded along the way by urgent

word and gesture, by shakings of her tail, and apos-
trophies most unreasonable.

"Go lang, you old snail! what you gormin' all over
the road for? Want to sleep here, do ye? Of all slow
critters ever I see, you 're the beat 'em; cold molasses
kin gallop, 'longside o' you."

Poor Molly did not understand this kind of thing
from one with whom she had been so friendly-intimate
as Bije. She made such haste as she could, poor beast,
and it was a great relief when she saw Brindle's horns
round the corner; for now, she had already learned
from experience, the hurry was over. Now she and
her bovine friend could take their way along the
grassy road, as slowly as any cow could wish. Bijah,
who had come panting along the road, breathless with
haste and repeated adjurations, became suddenly
compassionate. The poor beasts were tired, likely.
'T would n't do to hurry them; anyhow, 't was bad for
the cream. Oh, Bijah! Bijah! what would your pious
grandmother say, if she were witness of your bare-
faced duplicity on these occasions?

But what occasions they were! It was a pretty
sight, if one had been there to see. The road was
pretty, to begin with, — the Indiana road, with its
overhanging birches and elms, and the fringe of daisies
and golden-rod along the sides. The evening light was
soft and sweet, as if the sun had put on his tenderest
gleam to smile on Betsy; and as the twilight deep-

ened, in rosy gray softening into amethyst, did not the
moon come up, all clear and silver, just to look at
Betsy? The white light shimmered on the girl's soft
hair, and deepened the dimples in her round cheek,
and cast strange gleams into her lovely eyes. Was the
other Juliet fairer, I wonder? Possibly; but, on the
other hand, she could not drive cows, nor milk them,
either. Surely the other Romeo was not more passionate than this dark-eyed boy in his brown jean
overalls, walking so sedately by Juliet's — I should
say, by Betsy's — side. Bije felt as if the whole world
were light and fire; the fire within him, the light
without. He thought that Betsy gave light to the
moon, not the moon to Betsy. He did not wish he
were a glove upon that hand, for the little brown hand
had never worn a glove, except once, at the wedding
of a friend. The gloves were at home now, wrapped
in silver paper; she meant to wear them at her own
wedding. He did not swear by yonder blessed moon,
because he was not in the habit of swearing. "By
gosh!" was the only expletive Bije ever used, and he
would not have thought of using that in a lady's
presence. The fire within burned him; but what
sweet pain it was! If he had only had the gift of
language, this poor, dear Bije, what floods of glowing
words he would have poured out! How he would
have praised her, the beloved one, and praised the
night, and blessed the moon, and the stars, and the old

cows, and everything that came near him and his happiness! But if he had spoken, Bije could only have said that it was a sightly night, and Betsy would have responded that it was so.

One of these sightly nights Bijah found voice, if not language. They were pacing slowly along, letting Brindle and Molly have it all their own way. It was the full of the moon, the harvest-moon, and all the world lay bathed in silver light. They had been silent for a while, through sheer peace and content in each other; but suddenly Bije broke out with, " I wish 't I had a snow-apple!"

"Why, how you startled me!" Betsy responded. "Why do you want a snow-apple now, of all times in the world? They won't be ripe for nigh onto two months, Bije."

"Do you know what I thought of, first time ever I see you?" the boy went on, with apparent irrelevance. "Well, I thought of a snow-apple then, and thought you looked the most like one of anything in the world."

"Well, of all!" said Betsy.

"I did! There's nothing else as I know of that's so red and white, and so round, and so — so sweet, Betsy."

"Bijah Green, how you do talk!" Betsy cried. "It's time we was gettin' home with these cows." But she did not quicken her pace, and Bije noticed that she did not.

"Do you know what I'd do if you were a snow, Betsy?" Bije came a little nearer, and his voice grew husky.

"Eat me, presume likely!" said Betsy, with a little laugh that trembled as if it were full of tears.

"No!" cried the boy. "I'd pick you off the tree, though, and have you for my own, Betsy. I'd carry you off, and run away with you, sure's the world. Should — should you mind much, Betsy?"

But for once Betsy had nothing to say. She could only hang her head, and look more and more like the snow-apple, as Bije's arm stole round her, and his hand clasped hers. Little Betsy! She was only eighteen; four years older, it is true, than that creature of fire and perfume over in the other Verona, but still almost a child, according to New England ideas. The moon looked down, and probably thought she had seen the same sort of thing ever since she was an asteroid, and these children were like all the rest. But what a mistaken old moon she was, — for there had never been any one like Betsy, and certainly no one like Bijah, since the world began; and it was all perfectly new and strange, and — and — they had a very pleasant walk home.

"A bird of the air shall carry the matter!" What bird of all that fly could have had so bad a heart as to tell Miss Resigned Elizabeth of what was going on?

Did a raven come on heavy-flapping wings, and croak it in her ear? Or was it a magpie, or a chattering jay? Surely no respectable robin or oriole would think of such a thing! But, however the news reached her, it was there, and the golden time was rudely broken in upon.

Coming in one evening all flushed and radiant with her new joy, the child was met by her mistress (only we do not say "mistress" in New England; we say "she" or "her," as the case may be), — she was met, I say, by Miss Resigned Elizabeth, wearing so stern a face that the blush froze on Betsy's cheek, and the smile fled from the corners of her mouth, where it always loved to linger.

"Betsy Garlick, where have you been with that cow?"

Betsy faltered. "Been with her, Miss Bute? I've been bringing her back from pasture, same as I allers do."

"Same as you allers do? And how's that? Betsy Garlick, ain't you ashamed to look me in the face, and you goin' with that low-lived feller over t' the other house?"

But at this Betsy caught fire. "He ain't no low-lived feller!" she cried, the blushes coming back again in an angry flood over cheek and brow and neck. "You can scold me all you're a mind to, Miss Bute, and I won't say nothin'; but you ain't no call to abuse Bijah."

" Oh, I ain't, ain't I ? " cried Miss Resigned Elizabeth, taking fire in her turn. " I 'm to be shet up in my own house, am I, by a girl from North Beulah? I 'm to have such actions goin' on under my nose, and never so much as wink at 'em, am I ? I should like to know! You go to your room this minute, Betsy Garlick, and stay there till I tell you to come out, or you 'll find out p'raps more than you like. North Beulah! Well, of all impudence ! "

Betsy fled to her room, and the angry woman followed and turned the key upon her. Then, returning to her sitting-room, Miss Resigned Elizabeth sat down and made out her line of action in this domestic crisis. She sat for some time, her head shaking with indignation over the iniquities of this generation; then she went to the writing-desk, so seldom used, and, with stiff, trembling fingers, wrote two notes. One of the notes was posted, being intrusted to the care of the travelling baker, who went jingling by just in the nick of time; the other was thrust in at Miss Duty's door by a withered hand, which held it unflinchingly till Miss Duty came and took it, wondering greatly, but not opening the door an inch wider to catch a glimpse of her sister's face, — the face she had not looked into for ten years.

When the hand was withdrawn, Miss Duty proceeded to decipher the note, her gray hair bristling with indignation as she did so.

Sister Duty, — Your help has been courting my hired
girl, and I don't suppose you want any such doings, any
more than I do.   I have shet the girl up in her room till
he is gone, and sent for her stepmother.   So no more
from your sister,

R. E. Bute.

Who shall paint Miss Duty's wrath?   It was more
violent than her sister's, for she was of sterner mould;
and it was really a fiery whirlwind that greeted the
delinquent Bijah when he came whistling in from the
barn, cheerfully smiling and at peace with all the
world.   But the boy who faced Miss Duty in her fury
was a very different person from the meek, submissive
youth whom she had learned to know and tyrannize
over as Bije Green.

This Bije met her torrent of angry words with head
held high, and smiling countenance.   Ashamed?   No,
he was n't ashamed, not the least mite in the world.
Pick up his duds and go?   Why, of course he would —
just as easy!   Should he wait to split the kindling-
wood and bring in the water?   Just as she said; it
did n't make a mite o' difference to him.   Go right off,
this minute of time?   Ruther go than eat, any time.
One week's pay — thank her kindly, much obliged.
The cow was fed, and he cal'c'lated she'd find everything pretty slick in the barn.   Real pleasant night
for a walk — good evenin'!

The consequence of which was — what?   Certainly

5

not what Miss Duty had expected, or Miss Resigned, either.

At daybreak next morning, when the gray heads of these indignant virgins were still lying on their pillows, taking an interval of peace with all the world, Bijah was under Betsy's window, like a flame of fire. Betsy was not asleep. Oh, no! She was crying, poor little soul, at thought of going back to her stepmother, one of the old-fashioned kind, and never seeing Bije again. For she would never see him, of course. Hark! Was that a pebble thrown against the glass? A peep through the green blinds, up went the little window, softly, softly, and the dearest girl in the world leaned out, showing her sweet tear-stained face in the faint gray light, — a sight which made Bije more fiery than ever. Softly she bade him begone, for she dared not speak to him. How did he know Miss Bute was n't looking at him this minute, out of her window?

It appeared that Bije did not care if twenty Miss Butes were looking at him, though one was enough to frighten the crows. Betsy was to put on her bunnit that minute, and come along with him. Door locked? What did that matter, he should like to know? He should laugh if she was to be kept shet up there like a mouse in a trap. Send her home to her stepmother? He 'd like to see them try it, that was all. Never mind the things! Come right along! She 'd ben cryin'! He 'd like to get hold of them as made her cry. There 'd be *some* cryin' round, but it would n't be hers. Come! Why did n't Betsy come? They'd take the cows out to pasture this once more, — he did n't want the dumb critters to suffer, and 't was n't likely the old cats could get any help before night, — and then they'd go. Go where? Now Betsy knew that well enough. To Friar Laurence, of course (Bije called him parson instead of friar, and he spelled his name with a *w* instead of a *u*, but these are mere trifles of detail), to get married. Where else should they go? Was n't she his Betsy, his own girl? Did she think she was goin' to stay there and be hectored, while he was round? Parson Lawrence was to home, Bije saw him only last night. Now could she climb down that grape-vine? He reckoned she could, and he'd be standin' ready to catch her if her foot should slip.

"Oh, Bije! you take my breath away, you're so dretful speedy. Why, I can't — no way in the world. What — where should I go then, if — if we did — do what you say? Not that I can — with no clo'es but what I've got on. The idea!"

"Go? go home, of course, to mother's. Won't she be glad to see ye? Won't Delilah half eat ye up, she'll be so pleased? That's all you know, Betsy. And the help you'll be, and me too! Mother was dretful onreconciled to my goin' away, but I felt to go and see something of the world. And now I've seen all I want to, and I'm good and ready to go home, Betsy; but not alone."

How silver-sweet, indeed, sound lovers' tongues by night! But no sweeter than now in the early morning, when all the world was as young and fresh as Betsy, and as full of love and tenderness. In truth, it was the hour for a bridal. The air was full of bridal-veils: floating wreaths of silver fog that hung soft on the trees, and shimmered against the hill-sides, and here and there began to soften into golden and rosy tints as the light strengthened. They were all over the grass, too, these bridal-tokens, in tiny webs of purest spun-silver, diamond-set. A carpet of pearls was spread for Betsy's little feet, and she would never cry out, as slug-a-bed maidens do, if the pearls and diamonds wetted her shoes. Is the bride ready?

> " Red as a rose is she.
> Nodding their heads before her goes
> The merry minstrelsy."

Hark to them now! They are tuning their instruments in every branch of the elm-tree, cheep, twitter, trill; and now they burst out in a triumphal chorus of song: —

> " O Hymen, Hymenæe!"

and Betsy needs neither Mendelssohn nor Wagner to tell her what a wedding-march is. In very sooth, are there no young people beside Betsy and Bijah who know enough to be married in the early morning, and begin their first day together?

For Betsy can hold out no longer. She retires to

put on the pink calico gown, because Bije will not hear of her being married in any other. It is a pity that she will put on her best hat, instead of the pretty sun-bonnet; but one cannot expect a girl to be married in a "slat." She ties up her little bundle with trembling hands, while her cheeks glow and her heart beats so that she fancies Miss Bute must hear it in the room below.

Now she peeps out again, but shrinks back, afraid of the fire in the brown boy's eyes, and the passion of his outstretched arms. O Romeo! Romeo! But the whisper, "Betsy, *my* Betsy!" brings her out again, with a little proud, tearful smile. Yes, she is his Betsy. He is good and true; he will take care of her. She would trust all the world to Bijah.

Carefully now! The trellis is strong. (Had not Bijah tested it in the night, when she was sobbing in her sleep, to see that all was safe for her?) One foot on this round — so! Now down, slowly, carefully; take care of this step, for it is a weak one! Drop the bundle — there! Safe at last! At last! "All the world and we two," nothing else beside. As Betsy's foot touches the ground, up comes the sun to look at her. A long shaft of golden light touches her fair head, and lies like a benediction on her brow. The boy gazes at her, and sees no other sun. Ah, Juliet! if the measure of thy joy be heap'd like mine, and that thy skill be more to blazon it, then sweeten with thy

breath this neighbor air, and let rich music's tongue
unfold the imagin'd happiness that both receive in
either by this dear encounter. Call softly, though,
softly, so as not to wake the old ladies: "Co 'boss!
Co' boss!" Push the mossy gate, and let the good,
silent creatures out, the confidants of our love these
many weeks. Come, sweet Capulet! Come, Betsy,
and let us drive the cows to pasture!

Great was the wrath in the virgin bosoms of the
Misses Bute when the flight of Betsy and her dark-
eyed lover was discovered. Miss Duty relieved her
feelings by a furious bout of house-cleaning, and
scrubbed and scoured as if she were determined to
purge the house from the very memory of Bijah Green.
But Miss Resigned Elizabeth had a touch of rheumatism, and could not take refuge in that solace of
womankind. She could only sit and fret, poor soul,
and wish she had some one to talk it over with.
Dear to goodness! Come times like this, one did feel
forsaken. Miss Resigned Elizabeth almost felt that
she could make up with her sister, for the sake of the
common cause of anger they now had. She glanced
across the way, as she huddled up in her shawl, taking
the sun on the back-porch. If she had seen any softness in the lines of Miss Duty's back, as she stood
washing windows on her own porch, Miss Resigned
Elizabeth almost felt as if she could cough, or perhaps

even speak, just to pass the time of day. But Miss Duty's back was as rigid as her principles; and though she knew well enough that her sister was near, she gave no sign of consciousness. The younger sister felt forlorn and old, and drew her shawl closer around her, as if a ·cold air blew from that stiff figure on the other porch.

But 't was warmer here than in the house, anyway.

The house seemed strangely cold and cheerless since Betsy went away. There was no one singing in the little pantry, or making a cheerful clatter among the milk-pails. If Miss Resigned Elizabeth had only known how things were going to turn out, she would never have hired a girl; but now, it did n't seem as if she could get along without one, — coming winter, too.

But it was not so easy to get a girl in Verona. "Help is turrible skurce!" was the answer to all Miss Resigned Elizabeth's inquiries; nor did Miss Duty fare better in her search for a boy to fill the place of the delinquent Bijah. They both had to send for old John, the village chore-man, a surly elder, who grumbled bitterly at the half-mile walk on the Indiana road, and wanted to know what folks lived out there in the wilderness for, anyway. A sad time the poor ladies had now. Their pails were mixed up, because old John saw no reason for giving way to such foolishness on the part of the Bute girls, with whom he had gone to school forty years before, and who had

never been so all creation as they thought they were,
that he knew of. The indignant maidens found
baskets marked with hostile initials in the shed; and
if old John did not find what he wanted on the prem-
ises of one sister, he coolly took it from the other
house, without so much as "by your leave." They
could not even tell whether they were drinking their
own cow's milk, or that of the critter over'n the next
yard; for John drove the cows together to whichever
pasture he happened to fancy, and milked them together, whistling defiance as he did so. Any remonstrance was met with the announcement that he,
John, was only coming to accommodate, and the
sooner they found some one else to do their putterin',
the better he should be pleased.

It was really a dreadful state of things. Why, they
might almost as well be living together again, Miss
Duty thought; and Miss Resigned Elizabeth thought
so, too. And so the days wore on, and the weeks,
and made themselves into months; and the Misses
Bute mourned in secret for Betsy Garlick and Bijah
Green.

A year passed, as years do, whether people are comfortable or not. Miss Duty and Miss Resigned Elizabeth were not comfortable; but nobody seemed to
care, and help continued to be "turrible skurce."
Summer had come again, the late summer even, and
the harvest-moon. One evening, just at sunset, as

Miss Duty was straining the milk, there came a sharp knock at the door. Miss Duty did not altogether approve of people's knocking at her door at any time, and it was a special outrage just now, when anybody with brains in his head must know that she was busy; so she set down the pan and waited to see what would come next. Another knock came next, so imperious that Miss Duty wiped her hands on her apron and went to the door, outwardly calm, but inwardly raging.

There stood Calvin Parks, the driver of the Beulah stage, with a straw in his mouth and a twinkle in his eye.

"Lady out here to see you, Miss Bute," he said. "Very important business. Good evenin'!"

He was gone before the indignant lady could say a word. If you came to think of it, this was shameless impudence. A lady indeed! An agent, likely, selling some trash that was n't fit for stove-kindlings. At any rate, Miss Duty must go and give the woman a piece of her mind, comin' traipsin' round, just when folks was busy. The idea!

Out she went, fire in her eye, thunder ready rolling on her tongue. Out she went, and found — Betsy Garlick.

Betsy Green, rather; for the maiden Betsy never had this air of prosperity, this sweet, matronly look; was never dressed like this young woman, who sat on the boundary-stone that divided Miss Duty's lot from that of the other house, and smiled, — actually smiled in Miss Duty's face; and in her sister's too, for Calvin Parks had summoned Miss Resigned Elizabeth also, and she was approaching with feebler, slower steps. And who was this, standing by Betsy's side, erect, beaming, jubilant? Who but the recreant Bijah?

"Oh, Miss Butes!" cried Betsy, lifting her sweet face to one and then to the other of the sisters. "Please, Bijah and me could n't pass through Verony without stoppin' to pass the time of day, and see how you was gettin' on. We're real sorry we went off and left you that way, without notice. 'T wan't right, we know that now; but, then, we could n't find no other way to fix it, seemed 's though. I hope you don't bear malice, Miss Butes. We've done real well, Bijah and me. We're goin' now to look at a farm in Cortez 't we've heard of. Bijah's grandmother has left him quite consid'able of means, for us, and we want to have a place of our own, though no one could n't be kinder than Mother Green and Delilah has been. I — I hope you 've both been right smart, this time, and had good help right along?"

Oh, wicked little Betsy! You knew very well that they have *not* been right smart. Calvin Parks told you and Bijah all about their forlorn condition, and how old John bullied them (How did he know? Why, what is the use of being a stage-driver, if you do not

know everything ?), and you have come here with the
very slyest scheme in your little head that ever kindness and cleverness concocted. And now you are
going to play your trump-card, seeing that the two
ladies are still silent, each, perhaps, waiting for the
other to speak.

" And another reason we had for stoppin'," says
Betsy, looking down at a great bundle in her lap, from
which faint sounds now began to issue. "Oh, Miss
Butes, we — I *did* feel to have you see Baby, 'cause I
don't believe you ever did see such a darling in this
world." With these words, she drew the shawl aside,
and there on her lap lay the child, all warm and rosy,
just waking from his nap, and stretching his little
limbs, and blinking his eyes in the light.

A baby ! When had the Bute ladies seen a baby as
near as this ? Miss Resigned Elizabeth felt a tugging
at her heart-strings ; she had always been fond of
children. Miss Duty felt — she hardly knew what;
but she saw the tears on her sister's cheek ; saw, too,
how old and feeble she had grown, and what a pitiful
look there was in her pale blue eyes. And yet she
had a look of Mother, too !

At this moment the baby gave a crow and a kick,
and made a grab at Miss Duty's dress. In the effort,
he nearly rolled off his mother's lap. Instinctively
the two sisters bent down to catch him, and as they
did so their heads came together with a smart crack.

Miss Resigned Elizabeth began to cry, she could not tell why, and Miss Duty laughed. "You ain't fit to live alone, Resigned Eliz!" she said, and she hardly recognized her own voice.

"Well, I ain't, sister; that's a fact!" responded Miss Resigned Elizabeth, meekly. "My eyesight ain't what it was. But he _is_ a lovely child, Betsy; and — and I 'm right glad to see you, Betsy, if you _did n't_ act quite as you should."

"Why, you 're as blind as a mole!" cried the elder sister, in high good humor. "And you ain't had the sense to get glasses fitted." (Miss Duty could read the very smallest print, as well as she could twenty years ago) "The idea! And that thin dress ain't fit for you to wear this cold day." Miss Duty seemed to meditate. "Bije Green!" she said sharply, turning for the first time to her quondam "help"

"Yes, ma'am!" said Bije, meekly. He had kept silence till now, having absolute confidence in Betsy's diplomatic powers; but now he stepped boldly forward, and met Miss Duty's gaze without flinching.

"You behaved scandalous, Bije Green, when you was here before, as well you know. But I 'm willin' to let bygones be bygones, seein' things is how they is. You go get the wheelbarrow, and bring it here. Resigned 'Liz," she added, turning to her sister, " go on in, and pack up your things. I s'pose it 's fitting I should see to you, from now on. You come home, and we 'll

see. Mebbe I used to be a little cuterin', sometimes
— though you did try me."

"I know I did, sister!" Miss Resigned Elizabeth
cried. "Most prob'ly the fault was mine, though I did
feel your cuttin' up the hair bracelet. But there!
I 've been dretful lonesome sence Betsy went. I — I 'd
be real glad to come home, sister!"

"So that 's all there is to it," said Miss Duty, in a
final manner. "As for the other house —"

"Miss Bute!" cried Betsy Green, her eyes sparkling, her breath coming quickly. "We — we were n't
so dretful set on goin' to Cortez. We 'd enough sight
ruther find a place nearer home. I never thought —"
here she stopped short, being a truthful Betsy ; for she
had thought, and planned, and hoped in her kind little
heart, and now here was everything coming out just as
she hoped it would. "I 'd ruther live here than any-
where else in the world!" she said simply. "'T was
here I saw Bijah first, and all ; and you was real kind
to me, Miss Bute, and I do love Brindle."

"Them cows has been treated scand'lous," said Bije,
lifting up his testimony. "Whoever 's had the doin'
for 'em! All banged about, same as if the' was yaller
dogs. I took a look at 'em as we come along, and I
felt to pity 'em, now I tell you. I could take care of
'em, Miss Bute, jest as well as not, with what I had of
my own, and they would n't suffer none. I think a
sight of that red cow, and the other one, too."

"And I could do for both of you," cried Betsy, "all you 'd want done — me and Bije together. I could run over every mornin' and afternoon, and clean up if you was n't feelin' smart, and Bije could do the chores. And — and there 'd be Baby for company!" she added, with a little downward look of heavenly pride, — the very look, I declare, of a certain Bellini Madonna, who holds her lovely state in Venice. But now the baby thought his turn had come, and after a careful scrutiny of the two elderly women, he held out his arms and fairly shouted at Miss Resigned Elizabeth.

"You blessed creetur?" cried the poor woman, pouncing upon him with the pathetic hunger of a woman who was meant for a mother. "Did he want to come, bless his heart? Well, he should!" and she took the child up, and hugged and cuddled it "real knowin'," as Betsy said to herself. Miss Duty looked on in amazement. She had not the mother nature. "Why, Resigned 'Liz, you 're fairly childish. The idea!" She paused, feeling rebuked, she knew not why, by the joy in her sister's pinched and faded face. Miss Resigned Elizabeth had not had a joyous life.

"Well, if 't is to be so," Miss Duty continued, after a pause, during which Betsy and the younger sister held their breath and Bije thought about the cows. "If 't is to be so, so it will be, I s'pose. I dono' but you can go right in, Betsy, if it 's so you can stay. My sister ain't goin' to spend another night there. Perhaps you'll help her lay her things together. And Bije, if you feel to milk the cows to-night — I'm free to say I should like to send that John Peaslee about his business, after the hectorin' he's give us this late. You'll find the pails — "

But Bijah was already gone, whistling joyously. As if he didn't know where the milk-pails were!

"Betsy," Miss Duty continued, turning back to instruct the new tenant as to her course of action. But Betsy was gone, too; flown into the house with her baby, like a bird into its nest. Only Miss Resigned Elizabeth remained, looking at her with eyes that seemed to grow more plaintive and more helpless every minute, as the burden of responsibility dropped from her tired shoulders.

"You go right in the house this minute, Resigned 'Liz!" said Miss Duty, severely. "Gettin' your death out here in this night-air! The idea!" And with a frown that was better than a smile, she went into the house, driving her sister before her.

"A plague o' both your houses?" Nay! only joy on one side and the other of the white picket-fence. On the one side, content and peaceful days, with ten years' gossip to talk over, and the sense of being cared for, and of having "folks" once more. Happy old age coming softly, bringing with it grace and gentle words, and ways which their grim youth had never known; finally, the absolute rest which came from Betsy's and

Bijah's watchful love and care, and the strange pleasure of being called "aunt" by the baby, and the succeeding babies. Yes, the Bute girls were happy for the first time in their lives.

And on the other side of the fence? Ah! there it was not the calm peace of evening, but the fresh joy of morning and of spring. Seeing that there was no one in the world who could hold a candle to Bijah, and that Betsy was the best woman there was in these parts, let alone furrin lands, why should they not have been happy? And beside all this, had they not the most wonderful children, probably, that had ever been seen? There was not a doubt of it in Betsy's mind, nor in Miss Resigned Elizabeth's. Taking these things into consideration, together with the fact that their cows were most remarkable cows, and their hens the finest that had ever clucked in Verona, is it to be wondered at that our little friends were very happy, and the old ladies so good, and one of 'em an angel if she ever dared to call her soul her own?

A blessing on both houses! Peace and good-will, and all loving and tender thoughts! And may the sun, as he rises over the great hill-shoulder, always cast his brightest beams on the Indiana road.

THE END.